Bled Into Paper

A Collection of Poems on Grief

Alice Towe

BookLeaf Publishing

India | USA | UK

Dedication

To every soul navigating the wilderness of grief, may these words provide light along your path.

Preface

To anyone who has known loss, this collection of poems explores the many landscapes that grief inhabits - the deeply personal and the universally known. Within these pages you will hear the echoes of my own journey with that simultaneously pervasive shadow and warm light as it has shaped my life. It is my hope that you will recognize the contours of your own walk with grief and find solace in the shared language of sorrow and hope. May these poems invite moments of quiet contemplation, not to dwell on the pain, but to call to mind what remains after loss and what we gain from knowing it so intimately.

With Empathy - Thank you for reading.

Acknowledgements

To the Intrinsic Divine, my Great Love, my God, for always carrying me when I can no longer walk on my own two feet. To my family and friends, for their unwavering love, understanding, and patience as I have swam the waves of my ocean of grief.

I wish I had the words
to describe
the anguish in my bones,
the aching deep inside.

The changing in my soul,
An ebbing, flowing tide.

I wish I had the energy
to scream the way I need
to produce the sound
my spirit heaves.

To release the gasping panic
that comes from knowing grief.

The best way I can describe what I feel
is wild;
Wild with grief.
Primeval with loss.
Psychotic and consumed by all the love
I wanted to give.
Wading through an overflowing pool of all
the things I wanted to say and do.
It feels like drowning in the rapids of
love.
Or loss.
Or Time.

You can paint the walls
You can clean the room
You can take their calls
You won't shake the gloom.

You can wash the dishes
You can sweep the floor
Grief gives you wishes
That there was something more.

You can scream and cry
You can breathe so deep
You can get by
On very little sleep

You can binge, you can purge
You can barely eat
You'll survive on the urge
To play memories on repeat.

I wish that I could inside out
The way my heart outside ins.
I wish I knew beyond my doubts
That all the ends are all begins.

I hope that death is life beyond
The way that life beyonds to death,
And stretches too forever on
And has no need for beats and breaths.

There is something holy in the snow,
in the dead of winter,
in the Quiet.
God whispers on the wind to me
in this snow dusted field.
He thins the veil
between what I love and what I've lost,
and I see my father on the Other Side,
smiling and waving
in his favorite winter coat.
I smile and wave,
and watch him
in the Quiet.
Hot tears warm my cheeks,
kisses from him and
as close as we can get now —
for now.
In the Quiet
I contemplate what a gift grief is,
that love can reach so far
and be so close.
That on the coldest and snowiest of days,
it still finds us, and warms us,

if only for a few moments,
In the Quiet.

What do warriors do in times of peace?
How do they lay down their weapons,
their shields,
their arsenals of grief?
Are weapons a thing they can even
release?

Or do they kill aphids by the dozens?
And cripple caterpillars that decimate their
tomatoes.
Do they wrestle the garden hose to the
ground?
And swing an axe
for firewood
from a felled tree?

Maybe they lay beneath the stars at night
No shell — No booms — No need for fright.
And the crickets ask gently
for the armor they hold.
Do warriors hand over what made them so cold?
Is warmth a fire to survive
or a burning flame that hurts to hold?

It is a gift
To know grief —
A passport of your heart,
stamped with all the souls
you have loved
and lost.
A record for your swollen eyes
to review in between the dripping streams
of salt water that memories of them swim in.
It is a gift
To know grief.
All the names written on your heart —
A sacred incantation.
Your tears — the holy water that reminds you of those
blessings.
Your deep sighs —
the incense that roils over the pews of a blessed church
of memory.
It is a gift
To know grief.
How many years has it been?
You cannot measure love in time
because grief is not a pace, or a cadence,
or a ticking clock.

It is neither a tunnel to go through
nor a destination to reach.
Grief
is a gift
given by those who go on before you,
that you open on holidays, and quiet nights,
and while driving your car.
It is heavy to pick up
and painful to look at.
But it can a careful examination
of all the moments you shared —
a poignant reminder
of absence.
How powerful Love is,
that it is never lost –
only transformed
into a gift
for those who are brave enough to love —
and lose.

Hope isn't a logical thing —
It is a living thing.
It does not make sense that it is here;
That is survives —
Despite.
That is perseveres —
Regardless.
It breathes into the sick,
the weak,
the defeated.
It sews the stitches in the bleeding heart.
It laughs in the face of the conquered
alongside the once doubtful.
See?
It whispers.
You survived.
You won.
Let us go on fighting
another battle
another oppressor
another damned day.

I wonder
if you think I'm being dramatic.
I wonder
if you think I'm torturing myself,
counting down to the anniversary of when I lost the
person
I was most afraid of losing.
But you weren't there
in the thick of the battle.
You weren't begging God
or using all of your bargaining chips
for this one life.
You weren't in the car
at midnight
when I asked God to give me just a little
more time
and He said —
He already did.
You didn't hear the silence reverberate in my soul,
and you're not here
now
in my living room
where I sit in that same silence —
in that same car,

at that same time —
flashing back and forth
then and now,
and you can't see the difference
it has made
in my world
to be without him
yet another day.

Some days, I wither.
My life seems paper thin.
If I weep heavy, it stains the memories —
tears.
Some days, I absorb
every inch of light
and dark —
a swollen thing —
and pray for release.
Some days, I vacillate,
and can no more choose a word
than a lung can choose a breath;
(tremulous and indecisive)
compelled and inexorable.
Some days seem never ending;
a tunnel with no end.
I am a dresser crab, collecting as I go.
I am overwhelmed.
I am everything all at once;
too much and not enough —
full and insatiable —
the push and the pull
of wanting to be and hoping to
wither away.

I stepped into the wilderness of grief,
breathed deeply
and waited —
for the great catastrophe;
a barrage of blunt force pain —
but nothing came.

There was silence,
emptiness,
a hollow cave where a life once resided.

I was the only sound
of the wilderness.
The banshee's wail was no longer a scream to me;
I heard a familiar melody,
that bittersweet tune of loss and
I was not afraid any longer
of the beasts of grief
because I was one.

I am so exhausted by beauty
in the face of my grief.
Such comparable depth
that I ache doubly so.

And there has been occasions
where I cannot tell the difference.

And there has been occasions
where I do not think there is.

I see you

in the stain you used on the wooden shelves.

in the clothes you hung in the closet.

in the crisp mown lawn you manicured with love.

I hear you

in the creaks and groans of the house in the evening
wind.

in the rain tapping relentlessly on the tin roof in the
middle of the night.

in my very own laughter at the jokes you used to tell.

You are not with me

but you are with me all the time.

On the stormy days
When the air is quite electric,
hours before the downpour —
I am emptied —
hollowed out by grief,
by the lacking of your presence
in your favorite weather.
You would pull the attic door down
to better hear the rain on the tin roof;
to be immersed in the storm
but still held within the safety of this old house.
And I feel as if I, too, am in a storm,
searching to be immersed in you,
wanting after the safety of your walls.
But I am not within.
I am the house,
withstanding the storm,
the pelting rain, the torrent of wind,
the unstoppable downpour of the reality
that you're gone.
I creak and groan at the loss of you.
I am empty without your presence.

Come home.
Come rest your lonely bones.
Let me wash your war torn skin.
Feed you 'til you're whole again.
Come, come home.
Let me see how you've grown,
kiss every aching growing pain,
hold you in quiet refrain.
Come home, come home to me.
I'm waiting with your coffee,
with your favorite tea.
I've got breakfast on the table.
Come home to me,
if you're able.
In the meantime —
and every day —
I'll talk to your photo
until my grief goes away.

There is a room inside my heart
that once held the light of you.
Now when I visit, it is dark
and holds a lonely view.
I croon a melody of pain
Sadder than a mourning dove,
longing for you once again,
searching this room for your love.

Grief can silence me;
All the words I do not have are written on my heart.
Grief burns bright and wild in me;
I am a housefire hoping to be a phoenix.
Grief has held me sorrowful and sobbing;
It has been a cradle and a grave to the most tender parts
of me.
Grief has been the lifeline of my love;
the great unbroken thread of life and death.
Grief is the Great Love that walks along beside me
always;
a persevering force that can break me down,
and hold me steady.
Grief is the love that never leaves.

They did not tell me it would be so dark
to watch a loved one pass so far away.
The timeline difference would be so stark
I would not know the nighttime from the day.
The line drawn in the sand; the now, the then,
A mark so deeply carved in stone.
There is a moment when I will begin
to walk a brand new road all on my own.
A parallel to ev'rywhere Ive been,
repeating all the moves without the one -
the same old song and dance but missing them.
They do not mention grief is never done.
The do not mention grief is like the sun;
They do not tell you grief is never gone.

To love so deep that nothing comes between
To love so strong that nothing interrupts
A thread connecting throughout time, unseen
The force of something nothing can corrupt.
Remembering laughter you've yet to hear
Familiarity pure white and clean
The essence of a soul when it is near
I have only known few and far between
Recognition – a knowing that transcends
Reality. A knowing what has been,
The souls that you will walk with 'til the end.
It's nice to know we always meet again
Another time when we are diff'rent men.

I have seen you in so many places
Haunting across the house's wooden floor
Your stories in the creaks of this place is
A sound I hope will echo evermore.
I see you in the garden growing tall
The fruit of you on ev'ry branch and stem
I hear your laughter in a waterfall
I see you, healthy, swinging on a limb.
I saw you smiling in my smile today
I think I see you ev'rywhere I go
I hope that though you're gone, you always stay
So close to me that I will always know
That when I think it's you, it really is
That love does not depart, it always lives.

Notched in the doorway is a memory
'Neath boards of floor are notes I'll never read
The kitchen wafts aroma so gently
The fire in the hearth is all I need.
Outside there is a garden by the shed
That nourishes my soul and body, too
Back in the fields is where I buried dead
Where I have kept my heart so close to you
A simple life was all we ever asked
To work the land and live in quiet peace
To sleep beneath the starlight, oh we basked!
In home, in heart, in love that never ceased.
I visit with you when I feel alone
I know, one day, to you I will come home.